Table of Contents

P9-CAA-203

continued on next page

0-88012-455-5

continued from previous page

© 2006 Frank Schaffer Publications   0-88012-455-5

addition

Break the Spanish Code

Add each problem.
Find the letter in the code that corresponds to each answer.

9	8	9	4	3
8	7	7	7	5
6	5	6	2	6
5	4	4	5	8
3	2	3	2	2
2	1	2	8	4
1	0	5	7	6
4	3	0	6	8
9	8	7	4	0
+2	+1	+0	+1	+8

_____   _____   _____   _____   _____   *

code

a	36	e	43	m	13	s	36
b	49	f	57	n	46	t	38
c	42	g	60	o	50	u	39
d	41	h	51	p	54	v	34

Addition and Subtraction

Begin Step 1

1

0-88012-455-5

Addition and Subtraction

Find the sums.
Check by subtracting.

Here's an example

$$
\begin{array}{r} {}^{1}36 \\ +46 \\ \hline {}^{7}8\,{}^{1}2 \\ -46 \\ \hline 36 \end{array}
$$

$$
\begin{array}{r} 46 \\ +48 \\ \hline \end{array}
\qquad
\begin{array}{r} 57 \\ +24 \\ \hline \end{array}
\qquad
\begin{array}{r} 75 \\ +10 \\ \hline \end{array}
$$

$$
\begin{array}{r} 33 \\ +19 \\ \hline \end{array}
\qquad
\begin{array}{r} 42 \\ +29 \\ \hline \end{array}
\qquad
\begin{array}{r} 29 \\ +24 \\ \hline \end{array}
\qquad
\begin{array}{r} 25 \\ +28 \\ \hline \end{array}
$$

$$
\begin{array}{r} 64 \\ +26 \\ \hline \end{array}
\qquad
\begin{array}{r} 58 \\ +20 \\ \hline \end{array}
\qquad
\begin{array}{r} 74 \\ +18 \\ \hline \end{array}
\qquad
\begin{array}{r} 43 \\ +17 \\ \hline \end{array}
$$

2

0-88012-455-5

Addition and Subtraction

Find the sums.
Check by subtracting.

```
  1 1
  552
 + 78
 ─────
 5 12 1
  6̶3̶0̶
 - 78
 ─────
  552
```

```
    79
 + 834
```

```
   612
 +  99
```

```
   821
 +  69
```

```
    71
 + 641
```

```
    18
 + 905
```

```
    91
 + 642
```

```
   512
 +  98
```

```
    99
 + 852
```

3

  0-88012-455-5

Addition and Subtraction

Find the sums.
Check by subtracting.

Here's how

```
     1 1
      44
  + 3994
  ───────
  3 19
  4̶0̶3̶8̶
  - 3994
  ───────
      44
```

```
      81
  + 8675
  ───────
```

```
  7223
  +  13
  ───────
```

```
      42
  + 7274
  ───────
```

```
  5644
  +  58
  ───────
```

```
  4952
  +  26
  ───────
```

```
  9575
  +  76
  ───────
```

```
      65
  + 7523
  ───────
```

```
  6051
  +  86
  ───────
```

4

0-88012-455-5

Addition and Subtraction

Find the sums.
Check by subtracting.

```
 '3,'491          4,382          2,381
+3,758          +3,406         +4,653

 67'2'49
 7,249
-3,758
 3,491
```

```
 3,052           4,651          3,483
+4,487          +1,029         +5,259
```

```
 1,905           7,270          4,922
+2,184          +1,985         +1,487
```

5

    0-88012-455-5

addition

Addition

Find the sums.

359	684	142
427	322	601
+289	+715	+708

659	237	402
387	489	517
298	924	698
+315	+316	+224

791	857	247
842	228	482
604	929	379
217	118	804
+328	+308	+102

6

0-88012-455-5

Addition

Find the sums.

347	758	179
371	828	804
+497	+289	+642

513	137	104
892	419	571
378	124	324
+965	+361	+424

828	846	124
189	517	106
227	238	807
529	109	298
+408	+817	+715

7

 0-88012-455-5

Addition

Find the sums.

3,495	7,923	8,623
7,354	2,548	9,585
+6,372	+7,836	+2,434

4,646	3,497	6,486
9,733	4,315	3,327
3,875	9,572	8,715
+3,941	+1,385	+2,358

3,408	8,123	3,928
1,385	4,758	8,296
5,723	4,385	9,386
3,954	5,372	4,625
+3,976	+8,272	+1,821

8

  0-88012-455-5

Addition

Find the sums.

4,382	5,841	4,060
7,143	8,305	3,114
+2,176	+2,318	+2,379

9,186	7,602	1,135
4,239	4,864	2,259
6,319	1,729	6,822
+1,638	+3,821	+8,711

7,248	9,305	8,753
4,003	3,057	3,964
4,338	3,268	8,342
2,519	2,385	3,632
+6,350	+3,705	+4,632

9

0-88012-455-5

Making Change

Each shopper handed the checkout person a $20.00 bill. How much change did each receive?

$ 1.39	$ .45	$ .29
.59	.68	.88
2.09	.29	.42
.39	.99	3.45
.29	.89	6.18
.65	4.18	.23
.42	3.68	.59
1.48	.59	1.89
$.	.38	.29
tax .43	$.	$.
	tax .85	tax .90
total $.	total $.	total $.

change   change   change

$. $. $.

— .   — .   — .

$. $. $.

10

Subtraction

Find the differences.

35	50	54	85
−24	−27	−38	−16

546	998	367
−29	−15	−18

867	911	744
−288	−326	−575

4,357	5,738	7,352
−26	−92	−65

6,172	1,725	9,372
−3,081	−1,413	−3,741

3,448	8,779	6,760
−2,374	−5,137	−2,125

11

 0-88012-455-5

Break the French Code

Subtract each problem.
Find the letter in the code that corresponds to each answer.

527	822	1823	510
—452	—726	—976	—255

___   ___   ___   ___

931	483	1,215	1,252
—627	—291	—368	—928

*

___   ___   ___   ___

code							
a	634	e	847	l	720	m	436
i	192	o	555	n	324	r	96
u	721	b	304	s	255	t	75
c	82	f	266	w	177	d	999
h	452	k	161	g	883	j	111

12

0-88012-455-5

Subtraction

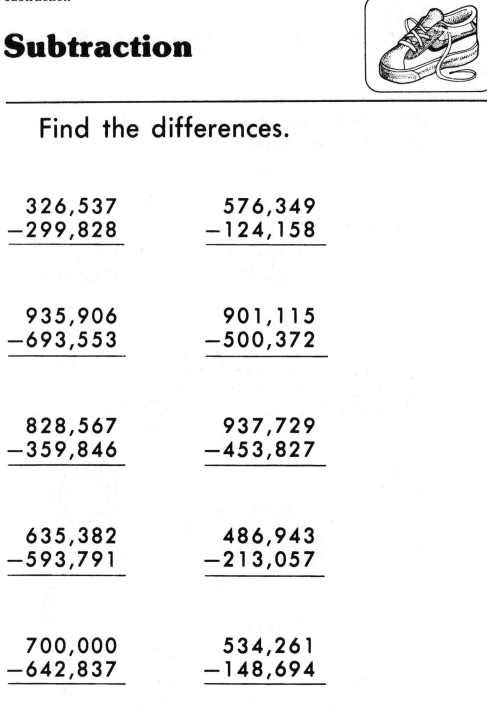

Find the differences.

326,537 −299,828	576,349 −124,158
935,906 −693,553	901,115 −500,372
828,567 −359,846	937,729 −453,827
635,382 −593,791	486,943 −213,057
700,000 −642,837	534,261 −148,694

13

 0-88012-455-5

On Sale Now!

How much can you save by waiting to buy each item on sale?

Reg. $38.97
Sale   24.79

$39.47 Reg.
29.98 Sale

$16.59
14.00

Reg. $22.50
Sale   18.79

$6.80
4.89

$35.88
30.99

$8.95
6.59

$4.85
2.69

Super Skate

tennis
balls

14

0-88012-455-5

Addition and Subtraction

Find the sums and differences.

```
  7,248           8,405
    651   4,537     236
+ 4,003  -2,519  +4,027
```

```
  7,005           3,468
    428  43,026  
+ 5,675   -219   -2,384
```

```
  9,648            437
     44   4,382     12
  +738    -761   +9,256
```

```
  843,753    1,834,216
+ 629,441   -1,772,105
```

15

 0-88012-455-5

Addition and Subtraction

Find the sums and differences.

```
    529
  4,604          3,118         3,421
 +4,060         -1,207         9,806
                              +3,349


  9,613
    382          9,893         5,008
 +1,834         -7,521        -4,201


    438
  9,511         90,006         8,462
   +473        -52,221           729
                                 +41


              763,821         871,135
             +937,265        +680,012
```

0-88012-455-5

Number Bank

The answers are given.

Figure out what the problems are by choosing the correct numerals from the bottom of the page.

$$
\begin{array}{r}
5\,5\,2 \\
+\ \underline{} \\
8\,1\,0
\end{array}
\qquad
\begin{array}{r}
3 \\
-\ \underline{} \\
2\,2\,3
\end{array}
\qquad
\begin{array}{r}
+\ \underline{1} \\
8\,9\,0
\end{array}
$$

$$
\begin{array}{r}
-\ \underline{5} \\
9\,2
\end{array}
\qquad
\begin{array}{r}
6 \\
+\ \underline{} \\
7\,7\,8
\end{array}
\qquad
\begin{array}{r}
-\ \underline{8} \\
3\,7\,5
\end{array}
$$

258	171	757
719	356	543
382	237	145
422	362	459
697	320	424

17

0-88012-455-5

Number Bank

The answers are given.

Figure out what the problems are by choosing the correct numerals from the bottom of the page.

```
   3 6 9            0
+  ___          + ___          -  ___  3
  6 0 3           5 9 5           7 7 2
```

```
                   4
-  ___  1       + ___          -  ___  6
  1 5 1           6 9 3           1 1 1
```

Congratulations!
You're finished
step one!

You have finished

Step 1

326	450	125
123	145	895
712	234	649
561	404	289
437	512	347

18

0-88012-455-5

Multiplication

How many stamps are in each sheet?

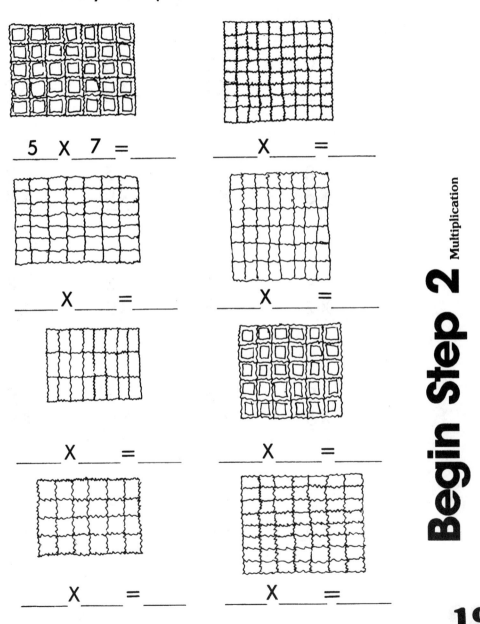

5 X 7 = ____

____ X ____ = ____

____ X ____ = ____

____ X ____ = ____

____ X ____ = ____

____ X ____ = ____

____ X ____ = ____

____ X ____ = ____

Begin Step 2 Multiplication

19

0-88012-455-5

Multiplication

Find the products.

0 X6	0 X1	6 X0	4 X0
8 X6	6 X6	5 X8	3 X8
9 X2	6 X8	3 X9	8 X9
9 X5	5 X7	1 X9	9 X9
7 X6	9 X8	8 X5	7 X4

20

 0-88012-455-5

Multiplication

Find the products.

7 X5	9 X3	9 X6	3 X1
5 X4	6 X6	2 X3	4 X7
6 X9	8 X7	2 X5	6 X8
8 X8	4 X3	7 X6	3 X6
1 X2	5 X8	4 X6	9 X7

21

0-88012-455-5

Multiplication

Find the products.

9 X1	7 X7	3 X2	1 X6	4 X9
0 X0	9 X6	6 X0	2 X0	4 X7
9 X9	7 X2	2 X5	5 X5	8 X1
4 X5	3 X4	0 X7	5 X9	3 X0
1 X8	7 X9	8 X6	5 X2	4 X4

22

0-88012-455-5

Multiplication

Find the products.

9 X8	4 X3	7 X4	9 X0	7 X5
0 X3	2 X1	9 X2	8 X4	1 X1
3 X9	7 X0	6 X7	6 X5	3 X5
4 X1	4 X6	6 X2	2 X2	1 X5
2 X9	5 X8	6 X3	0 X9	1 X4

23

 0-88012-455-5

Multiplication

Find the products.

an example

$$
\begin{array}{r}
{\scriptstyle 2} \\
24 \\
\times 6 \\
\hline
144
\end{array}
$$

$$
\begin{array}{r}
48 \\
\times 7 \\
\hline
\end{array}
\qquad
\begin{array}{r}
63 \\
\times 5 \\
\hline
\end{array}
\qquad
\begin{array}{r}
53 \\
\times 9 \\
\hline
\end{array}
$$

$$
\begin{array}{r}
29 \\
\times 4 \\
\hline
\end{array}
\qquad
\begin{array}{r}
79 \\
\times 3 \\
\hline
\end{array}
\qquad
\begin{array}{r}
45 \\
\times 3 \\
\hline
\end{array}
\qquad
\begin{array}{r}
57 \\
\times 6 \\
\hline
\end{array}
$$

$$
\begin{array}{r}
84 \\
\times 6 \\
\hline
\end{array}
\qquad
\begin{array}{r}
43 \\
\times 6 \\
\hline
\end{array}
\qquad
\begin{array}{r}
50 \\
\times 3 \\
\hline
\end{array}
\qquad
\begin{array}{r}
30 \\
\times 5 \\
\hline
\end{array}
$$

$$
\begin{array}{r}
36 \\
\times 4 \\
\hline
\end{array}
\qquad
\begin{array}{r}
48 \\
\times 4 \\
\hline
\end{array}
\qquad
\begin{array}{r}
57 \\
\times 3 \\
\hline
\end{array}
\qquad
\begin{array}{r}
32 \\
\times 5 \\
\hline
\end{array}
$$

$$
\begin{array}{r}
88 \\
\times 2 \\
\hline
\end{array}
\qquad
\begin{array}{r}
64 \\
\times 9 \\
\hline
\end{array}
\qquad
\begin{array}{r}
43 \\
\times 8 \\
\hline
\end{array}
\qquad
\begin{array}{r}
33 \\
\times 7 \\
\hline
\end{array}
$$

24

 0-88012-455-5

Multiplication

Find the products.

32 X7	63 X2	87 X5	94 X2
56 X0	47 X9	77 X6	40 X3
36 X8	54 X1	27 X4	84 X6
16 X7	62 X3	76 X5	92 X4

25

Multiplication

Find the products.

97 X8	48 X6	15 X1	29 X8
61 X5	97 X9	36 X2	57 X7
51 X7	95 X3	35 X5	13 X9
28 X4	48 X8	83 X6	74 X4

26

0-88012-455-5

Multiplication

Find the products.

$$
\begin{array}{r} {}^{2\ 4}725 \\ \times 8 \\ \hline 5,800 \end{array}
\qquad
\begin{array}{r} 642 \\ \times 9 \\ \hline \end{array}
\qquad
\begin{array}{r} 204 \\ \times 3 \\ \hline \end{array}
$$

$$
\begin{array}{r} 106 \\ \times 9 \\ \hline \end{array}
\qquad
\begin{array}{r} 754 \\ \times 4 \\ \hline \end{array}
\qquad
\begin{array}{r} 615 \\ \times 7 \\ \hline \end{array}
$$

$$
\begin{array}{r} 781 \\ \times 4 \\ \hline \end{array}
\qquad
\begin{array}{r} 502 \\ \times 8 \\ \hline \end{array}
\qquad
\begin{array}{r} 225 \\ \times 8 \\ \hline \end{array}
$$

$$
\begin{array}{r} 514 \\ \times 6 \\ \hline \end{array}
\qquad
\begin{array}{r} 154 \\ \times 6 \\ \hline \end{array}
\qquad
\begin{array}{r} 369 \\ \times 3 \\ \hline \end{array}
$$

27

Multiplication

Find the products.

Here's how

$$
\begin{array}{r}
\overset{2\;6}{9}27 \\
\times 9 \\
\hline
8{,}343
\end{array}
$$

$$
\begin{array}{r}
846 \\
\times 5 \\
\hline
\end{array}
\qquad
\begin{array}{r}
902 \\
\times 3 \\
\hline
\end{array}
$$

$$
\begin{array}{r}
610 \\
\times 4 \\
\hline
\end{array}
\qquad
\begin{array}{r}
297 \\
\times 2 \\
\hline
\end{array}
\qquad
\begin{array}{r}
306 \\
\times 6 \\
\hline
\end{array}
$$

$$
\begin{array}{r}
715 \\
\times 7 \\
\hline
\end{array}
\qquad
\begin{array}{r}
115 \\
\times 8 \\
\hline
\end{array}
\qquad
\begin{array}{r}
512 \\
\times 1 \\
\hline
\end{array}
$$

$$
\begin{array}{r}
915 \\
\times 3 \\
\hline
\end{array}
\qquad
\begin{array}{r}
139 \\
\times 4 \\
\hline
\end{array}
\qquad
\begin{array}{r}
721 \\
\times 5 \\
\hline
\end{array}
$$

28

 0-88012-455-5

Multiplication

Find the products.

517 X6	344 X8	628 X9
473 X3	246 X8	163 X4
438 X2	646 X9	728 X8
743 X9	416 X7	400 X8
399 X1	755 X8	807 X2

29

0-88012-455-5

Multiplication

Find the products.

Your example

87 X25 435 174 2,175	43 X24	68 X71

57 X44	70 X38	88 X14

27 X16	46 X53	76 X92

33 X47	86 X24	43 X16

30

0-88012-455-5

Multiplication

Find the products.

```
   45        45        45        45
  X32       X32       X32       X32
             90        90        90
                      135       135
                               1440
```

We did this one for you

```
   36        42        18
  X15       X25       X37
```

```
   65        11        28
  X24       X54       X11
```

31

0-88012-455-5

Multiplication

Find the products.

Here's how

37	37	37	37
X84	X84	X84	X84
	148	148	148
		296	296
			3,108

```
  49        19        56
X38       X48       X61
```

```
  65        19        98
X22       X49       X12
```

0-88012-455-5

Multiplication

Find the products.

```
 457    457    457    457
X34    X34    X34    X34
       1828   1828   1828
              1371   1371
                    15,538
```

```
524    351    724
X38    X65    X49
```

```
648    472    438
X89    X84    X95
```

    0-88012-455-5

Multiplication

Find the products.

```
 364      364      364       364
X 45     X 45     X 45      X 45
         1820     1820      1820
                  1456      1456
                           16,380
```

```
 367      211      744
X 88     X 26     X 75
```

```
 682      553      861
X 95     X 64     X 44
```

34

0-88012-455-5

Multiplication

Find the products.

```
  615      615      615      615      615
 X276     X276     X276     X276     X276
          3690     3690     3690     3690
                   4305     4305     4305
                            1230     1230
                                   169,740
```

Study this first

```
   313        622        220
  X478       X269       X178
```

```
   946        431        530
  X148       X278       X467
```

35

   0-88012-455-5

Multiplication

Find the products.

an example

```
 943    9̇4̇3    9̇4̇3    9̇4̇3     943
X269   X269   X269   X269   X269
8487   8487   8487   8487   8487
              5658   5658   5658
                     1886   1886
                           253,667
```

```
  942        860        611
X172       X279       X176
```

```
  330        811        419
X295       X189       X514
```

0-88012-455-5

Multiplication

Find the products.

56	787	1,576
X8	X9	X7

68	362	4,921
X42	X81	X52

379	5,124
X482	X359

0-88012-455-5

Multiplication

Find the products.

$$\begin{array}{r} 48 \\ \times 5 \\ \hline \end{array} \qquad \begin{array}{r} 653 \\ \times 7 \\ \hline \end{array} \qquad \begin{array}{r} 2,134 \\ \times 4 \\ \hline \end{array}$$

$$\begin{array}{r} 32 \\ \times 24 \\ \hline \end{array} \qquad \begin{array}{r} 604 \\ \times 88 \\ \hline \end{array} \qquad \begin{array}{r} 3,011 \\ \times 79 \\ \hline \end{array}$$

$$\begin{array}{r} 789 \\ \times 857 \\ \hline \end{array} \qquad \begin{array}{r} 4,070 \\ \times 305 \\ \hline \end{array}$$

38

 0-88012-455-5

Multiplication

Find the products.

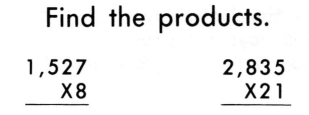

$$
\begin{array}{r}
1,527 \\
\times 8 \\
\hline
\end{array}
\qquad
\begin{array}{r}
2,835 \\
\times 21 \\
\hline
\end{array}
$$

$$
\begin{array}{r}
8,652 \\
\times 341 \\
\hline
\end{array}
\qquad
\begin{array}{r}
1,437 \\
\times 481 \\
\hline
\end{array}
$$

$$
\begin{array}{r}
5,642 \\
\times 9,831 \\
\hline
\end{array}
\qquad
\begin{array}{r}
7,502 \\
\times 1,346 \\
\hline
\end{array}
$$

39

Hours, Days, and Years

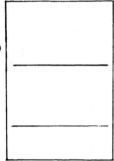

1. 24 hours in a day.
   365 days in a year.
   How many hours in a year?

2. How many hours in
   100 years?

3. How many more years to make about
   1,000,000 hours?

Well done!

You have finished

Step 2

4. About how many years equal 1,000,000
   hours? _____

40

0-88012-455-5

One Number Puzzle

Multiply going across.
Divide going down.

8	x	3	x	2	=	
÷	■	÷	■	÷	■	÷
2	x	1	x	1	=	
÷	■	÷	■	÷	■	÷
2	x	3	x	2	=	
=	■	=	■	=	■	=
	x		x		=	

Begin Step 3 Division

0-88012-455-5

One Number Puzzle

Multiply going across.
Divide going down.

4	x	2	x	4	=	
÷	■	÷	■	÷	■	÷
1	x	1	x	1	x	
÷	■	÷	■	÷	■	÷
4	x	2	x	1	=	
=	■	=	■	=	■	=
	x		x		=	

42

0-88012-455-5

TUTOR'S GUIDE
Mathematics Level 4

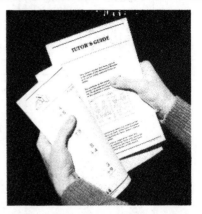

This answer section has been placed in the center of this Homework Booklet so it can be easily removed if you so desire.

The solutions in this manual reflect the layout of the exercises to simplify checking. The problem solving process as well as the solution is shown.

page 1

9	8	9	4	3
8	7	7	7	5
6	5	6	2	6
5	4	4	5	8
3	2	3	2	2
2	1	2	8	4
1	0	5	7	6
4	3	0	6	8
9	8	7	4	0
+2	+1	+0	+1	+8
49	39	43	46	50
b	u	e	n	o

code

o	36	e	43	m	13	‹	36
b	49	f	57	n	46	ı	38
c	42	g	60	o	50	u	39
d	41	h	51	p	54	v	34

*Spanish for, "Good"!

page 2

$$\begin{array}{c} 36 \\ +46 \\ \hline \end{array} \quad \begin{array}{c} 46 \\ +48 \\ \hline \end{array} \quad \begin{array}{c} 57 \\ +24 \\ \hline \end{array} \quad \begin{array}{c} 75 \\ +10 \\ \hline \end{array}$$

$$\begin{array}{c} 82 \\ -46 \\ \hline 36 \end{array} \quad \begin{array}{c} 94 \\ -48 \\ \hline 46 \end{array} \quad \begin{array}{c} 81 \\ -24 \\ \hline 57 \end{array} \quad \begin{array}{c} 85 \\ -10 \\ \hline 75 \end{array}$$

$$\begin{array}{c} 33 \\ +19 \\ \hline \end{array} \quad \begin{array}{c} 42 \\ +29 \\ \hline \end{array} \quad \begin{array}{c} 29 \\ +24 \\ \hline \end{array} \quad \begin{array}{c} 25 \\ +28 \\ \hline \end{array}$$

$$\begin{array}{c} 52 \\ -19 \\ \hline 33 \end{array} \quad \begin{array}{c} 71 \\ -29 \\ \hline 42 \end{array} \quad \begin{array}{c} 53 \\ -24 \\ \hline 29 \end{array} \quad \begin{array}{c} 53 \\ -28 \\ \hline 25 \end{array}$$

$$\begin{array}{c} 64 \\ +26 \\ \hline \end{array} \quad \begin{array}{c} 58 \\ +20 \\ \hline \end{array} \quad \begin{array}{c} 74 \\ +18 \\ \hline \end{array} \quad \begin{array}{c} 43 \\ +17 \\ \hline \end{array}$$

$$\begin{array}{c} 90 \\ -26 \\ \hline 64 \end{array} \quad \begin{array}{c} 78 \\ -20 \\ \hline 58 \end{array} \quad \begin{array}{c} 92 \\ -18 \\ \hline 74 \end{array} \quad \begin{array}{c} 60 \\ -17 \\ \hline 43 \end{array}$$

A motivational award is provided on the inside back cover. It has been designed to be signed by the tutor, either a parent or teacher.

Motivational suggestion: After the student completes each step, mark the achievement by placing a sticker next to that step shown on the award.

0-88012-455-5

Solutions

page 3

552 +78 **630** −78 552	79 +834 **913** −834 79	612 +99 **711** −99 612
821 +69 **890** −69 821	71 +641 **712** −641 71	18 +905 **923** −905 18
91 +642 **733** −642 91	512 +98 **610** −98 512	852 +852 **951** −852 99

page 4

44 +3994 **4038** −3,994 44	81 +8675 **8,756** −8,675 81	7223 +13 **7,236** −13 7,223
42 +7274 **7,316** −7,274 42	5644 +58 **5702** −58 5644	4952 +26 **4,978** −26 4,952
9575 +76 **9,651** −76 9,575	65 +7523 **7588** −7,523 65	6051 +86 **6,137** −86 6051

page 5

3,491 +3,758 **7,249** −3,758 3,491	4,382 +3,406 **7,788** −3,406 4,382	2,381 +4,653 **7,034** −4,653 2,381
3,052 +4,487 **7,539** −4,487 3,052	4,651 +1,029 **5,680** −1,029 4,651	3,483 +5,259 **8,742** −5,259 3,483
1,905 +2,184 **4,089** −2,184 1,905	7,270 +1,985 **9,255** −1,985 7,270	4,922 +1,487 **6,409** −1,487 4,922

page 6

359 427 +289 **1,075**	684 322 +715 **1,721**	142 601 +708 **1,451**
659 387 298 +315 **1,659**	237 489 924 +316 **1,966**	402 517 698 +224 **1,841**
791 842 604 217 +328 **2,782**	857 228 929 118 +308 **2,440**	247 482 379 804 +102 **2,014**

page 7

347 371 +497 **1,215**	758 828 +289 **1,875**	179 804 +642 **1,625**
513 892 378 +965 **2,748**	137 419 124 +361 **1,041**	104 571 324 +424 **1,423**
828 189 227 529 +408 **2,181**	846 517 238 109 +817 **2,527**	124 106 807 298 +715 **2,050**

page 8

3,495 7,354 +6,372 **17,221**	7,923 2,548 +7,836 **18,307**	8,623 9,585 +2,434 **20,642**
4,646 9,733 3,875 +3,941 **22,195**	3,497 4,315 9,572 +1,385 **18,769**	6,486 3,327 8,715 +2,358 **20,886**
3,408 1,385 5,723 3,954 +3,976 **18,446**	8,123 4,758 4,385 5,372 +8,272 **30,910**	3,928 8,296 9,386 4,625 +1,821 **28,056**

page 9

4,382 7,143 +2,176 **13,701**	5,841 8,305 +2,318 **16,464**	4,060 3,114 +2,379 **9,553**
9,186 4,239 6,319 +1,638 **21,382**	7,602 4,864 1,729 +3,821 **18,016**	1,135 2,259 6,822 +8,711 **18,927**
7,248 4,003 4,338 2,519 +6,350 **24,458**	9,305 3,057 3,268 2,385 +3,705 **21,720**	8,753 3,964 8,342 3,632 +4,632 **29,323**

page 10

$ 1.39 .59 2.09 .39 .29 .65 .42 1.48 tax .43 total $ 7.73	$ .45 .68 .29 .99 .89 4.18 3.68 .59 .38 $ 12.13 tax .85 total $ 12.98	$ .29 .88 .42 3.45 6.18 .23 .59 1.89 .29 $ 14.22 tax .90 total $ 15.12
change $ 20.00 − 7.73 $ 12.27	change $ 20.00 − 12.98 $ 7.02	change $ 20.00 − 15.12 $ 4.88

page 11

35 −24 **11**	50 −27 **23**	84 −38 **16**	85 −16 **69**
546 −29 **517**	998 −15 **983**	367 −18 **349**	
867 −288 **579**	911 −326 **585**	744 −575 **169**	
4,357 −26 **4,331**	5,738 −92 **5,646**	7,352 −65 **7,287**	
6,172 −3,081 **3,091**	1,725 −1,413 **312**	9,372 −3,741 **5,631**	
3,448 −2,374 **1,074**	8,779 −5,137 **3,642**	6,760 −2,125 **4,635**	

page 12

527 −452 **75**	822 −726 **96**	1823 −976 **847**	510 −255 **255**

t r e s

931 −627 **304**	483 −291 **192**	1,215 −368 **847**	1,252 −928 **324**

b i e n

code			
a 634	e 847	l 720	m 436
i 192	o 555	n 324	r 96
u 721	b 304	s 255	t 75
c 82	f 266	w 177	d 999
h 452	k 161	g 883	j 111

*French for, "Very good"!

page 13

326,537 −299,828 **26,709**	576,349 −124,158 **452,191**
935,906 −693,553 **242,353**	901,115 −500,372 **400,743**
828,567 −359,846 **468,721**	937,729 −453,827 **483,902**
635,382 −593,791 **41,591**	486,943 −213,057 **273,886**
700,000 −642,837 **57,163**	534,261 −148,694 **385,567**

page 14

Reg. $38.97 Sale 24.79 **$14.18**

$39.47 Reg. 29.98 Sale **$9.99**

Reg. $372.50 Sale 18.79 **$3.71**

$16.59 14.00 **$2.59**

$6.80 4.89 **$1.91**

$35.88 30.99 **$4.89**

$8.95 6.59 **$2.36**

$4.85 2.69 **$2.16**

0-88012-455-5

page 15

```
  7,248        4,537        8,405
    651       -2,519         236
+ 4,003                  + 4,027
 11,902        2,018       12,668

  7,005       43,026        3,468
    428         -219       -2,384
+ 5,675
 13,108       42,807        1,084

  9,648        4,382          437
     44         -761           12
  + 738                   + 9,256
 10,430        3,621        9,705

   843,753     1,834,216
 + 629,441    -1,772,105
 1,473,194        62,111
```

page 16

```
    529        8,118        3,421
  4,604       -1,207        9,806
+ 4,060                   + 3,349
  9,193        1,911       16,576

  9,613        9,893        5,008
    382       -7,521       -4,201
+ 1,834
 11,829        2,372          807

    438       98,806        8,462
  9,511      -52,221          729
  + 473                      + 41
 10,422       37,785        9,232

   763,821     871,135
 + 937,265   + 680,012
 1,701,086   1,551,147
```

page 17

```
  552        543        719
+ 258      - 320      + 171
  810        223        890

  237        356        757
  145      + 422      - 382
   92        778        375

  288        171        257
  219        395        543
  387        297        115
  427        362        459
  697        320        424
```

page 18

```
  369        450        895
+ 234      + 145        123
  603        595        772

  712        404        437
  561      + 289      - 326
  151        693        111

  375        450        125
  125        345        895
  217        234        649
  561        405        289
  437        512        347
```

page 19

```
5 x 7 = 35      8 x 9 = 72

7 x 7 = 49      6 x 8 = 48

3 x 8 = 24      5 x 6 = 30

4 x 6 = 24      8 x 7 = 56
```

page 20

```
  0      0      6      4
 X6     X1     X0     X0
  0      0      0      0

  8      6      5      3
 X6     X6     X8     X8
 48     36     40     24

  9      6      3      8
 X2     X8     X9     X9
 18     48     27     72

  9      5      1      9
 X5     X7     X9     X9
 45     35      9     81

  7      9      8      7
 X6     X8     X5     X4
 42     72     40     28
```

page 21

```
  7      9      9      3
 X5     X3     X6     X1
 35     27     54      3

  5      6      2      4
 X4     X6     X3     X7
 20     36      6     28

  6      8      2      6
 X9     X7     X5     X8
 54     56     10     48

  8      4      7      3
 X8     X3     X6     X6
 64     12     42     18

  1      5      4      9
 X2     X8     X6     X7
  2     40     24     63
```

page 22

```
  9      7      3      1      4
 X1     X7     X2     X6     X9
  9     49      6      6     36

  0      9      6      2      4
 X0     X6     X0     X0     X7
  0     54      0      0     28

  9      7      2      5      8
 X9     X2     X5     X5     X1
 81     14     10     25      8

  4      3      6      5      3
 X5     X4     X7     X9     X0
 20     12      0     45      0

  1      7      8      5      4
 X8     X9     X6     X2     X4
  8     63     48     10     16
```

page 23

```
  9      4      7      9      7
 X8     X3     X4     X0     X5
 72     12     28      0     35

  0      2      9      8      1
 X3     X1     X2     X4     X1
  0      2     18     32      1

  3      7      6      6      3
 X9     X0     X7     X5     X5
 27      0     42     30     15

  4      4      6      2      1
 X1     X6     X2     X2     X5
  4     24     12      4      5

  2      5      6      0      1
 X9     X8     X3     X9     X4
 18     40     18      0      4
```

page 24

```
  24     48     63     53
 X6     X7     X5     X9
 144    336    315    477

  29     79     45     57
 X4     X3     X3     X6
 116    237    135    342

  84     43     50     30
 X6     X6     X3     X5
 504    258    150    150

  36     48     57     32
 X4     X4     X3     X5
 144    192    171    160

  88     64     43     33
 X2     X9     X8     X7
 176    576    344    231
```

page 25

```
  32     63     87     94
 X7     X2     X5     X2
 224    126    435    188

  56     47     77     40
 X0     X9     X6     X3
   0    423    462    120

  36     54     27     84
 X8     X1     X4     X6
 288     54    108    504

  16     62     76     92
 X7     X3     X5     X4
 112    186    380    368
```

page 26

```
  87     48     15     29
 X8     X6     X1     X8
 776    288     15    252

  61     97     36     57
 X5     X9     X2     X7
 305    873     72    399

  51     95     35     13
 X7     X3     X5     X9
 357    285    175    117

  28     48     83     74
 X4     X8     X6     X4
 112    384    498    296
```

Solutions

0-88012-455-5

Solutions

0-88012-455-5

---

page 27

642 ×9 = 5,778	204 ×3 = 612	
106 ×9 = 954	754 ×4 = 3,016	615 ×7 = 4,305
781 ×4 = 3,124	502 ×8 = 4,016	225 ×8 = 1,800
514 ×6 = 3,084	154 ×6 = 924	369 ×3 = 1,107

page 28

846 ×5 = 4,230	902 ×3 = 2,706	
610 ×4 = 2,440	297 ×2 = 594	306 ×6 = 1,836
715 ×7 = 5,005	115 ×8 = 920	512 ×1 = 512
915 ×3 = 2,745	139 ×4 = 556	721 ×5 = 3,605

page 29

517 ×6 = 3,102	344 ×8 = 2,752	628 ×9 = 5,652
473 ×3 = 1,419	246 ×8 = 1,968	163 ×4 = 652
438 ×2 = 876	646 ×9 = 5,814	728 ×8 = 5,824
743 ×9 = 6,687	416 ×7 = 2,912	400 ×8 = 3,200
399 ×1 = 399	755 ×8 = 6,040	807 ×2 = 1,614

---

page 30

87 ×25 → 435 / 174 / 2,175	43 ×24 → 172 / 86 / 1,032	68 ×71 → 68 / 476 / 4,828
57 ×44 → 228 / 228 / 2,508	70 ×38 → 560 / 210 / 2,660	88 ×14 → 352 / 88 / 1,232
27 ×16 → 162 / 27 / 432	46 ×53 → 138 / 230 / 2,438	76 ×92 → 152 / 684 / 6,992
33 ×47 → 231 / 132 / 1,551	86 ×24 → 344 / 172 / 2,064	43 ×16 → 258 / 43 / 688

page 31

| 36 ×15 → 180 / 36 / 540 | 42 ×25 → 210 / 84 / 1,050 | 18 ×37 → 126 / 54 / 666 |
| 65 ×24 → 260 / 130 / 1,560 | 11 ×54 → 44 / 55 / 594 | 28 ×11 → 28 / 28 / 308 |

page 32

| 49 ×38 → 392 / 147 / 1,862 | 19 ×48 → 152 / 76 / 912 | 56 ×61 → 56 / 336 / 3,416 |
| 65 ×22 → 130 / 130 / 1,430 | 19 ×49 → 171 / 76 / 931 | 98 ×12 → 196 / 98 / 1,176 |

---

page 33

| 524 ×38 → 4192 / 1572 / 19,912 | 351 ×65 → 1755 / 2106 / 22,815 | 724 ×49 → 6516 / 2896 / 35,476 |
| 648 ×89 → 5832 / 5184 / 57,672 | 472 ×84 → 1888 / 3776 / 39,648 | 438 ×95 → 2190 / 3942 / 41,610 |

page 34

| 367 ×88 → 2936 / 2936 / 32,296 | 211 ×26 → 1266 / 422 / 5,486 | 744 ×75 → 3720 / 5208 / 55,800 |
| 682 ×95 → 3410 / 6138 / 64,790 | 553 ×64 → 2212 / 3318 / 35,392 | 861 ×44 → 3444 / 3444 / 37,884 |

page 35

| 313 ×478 → 2504 / 2191 / 1252 / 149,614 | 622 ×269 → 5598 / 3732 / 1244 / 167,318 | 220 ×178 → 1760 / 1540 / 220 / 39,160 |
| 946 ×148 → 7568 / 3784 / 946 / 140,008 | 431 ×278 → 3448 / 3017 / 862 / 119,818 | 530 ×467 → 3710 / 3180 / 2120 / 247,510 |

---

page 36

| 942 ×172 → 1884 / 6594 / 942 / 162,024 | 860 ×279 → 7740 / 6020 / 1720 / 239,940 | 611 ×176 → 3666 / 4277 / 611 / 107,536 |
| 330 ×295 → 1650 / 2970 / 660 / 97,350 | 811 ×189 → 7299 / 6488 / 811 / 153,279 | 419 ×514 → 1676 / 419 / 2095 / 215,366 |

page 37

56 ×8 = 448	787 ×9 = 7,083	1,576 ×7 = 11,032
68 ×42 → 136 / 272 / 2,856	362 ×81 → 362 / 2896 / 29,322	4,921 ×52 → 9842 / 24605 / 255,892
379 ×482 → 758 / 3032 / 1516 / 182,678		5,124 ×359 → 46116 / 25620 / 15372 / 1,839,516

page 38

48 ×5 = 240	653 ×7 = 4,571	2,134 ×4 = 8,536
32 ×24 → 128 / 46 / 768	604 ×88 → 4832 / 4832 / 53,152	3,011 ×79 → 27099 / 21077 / 237,869
789 ×857 → 5523 / 3945 / 6312 / 676,173		4,070 ×305 → 20350 / 00000 / 12210 / 1,241,350

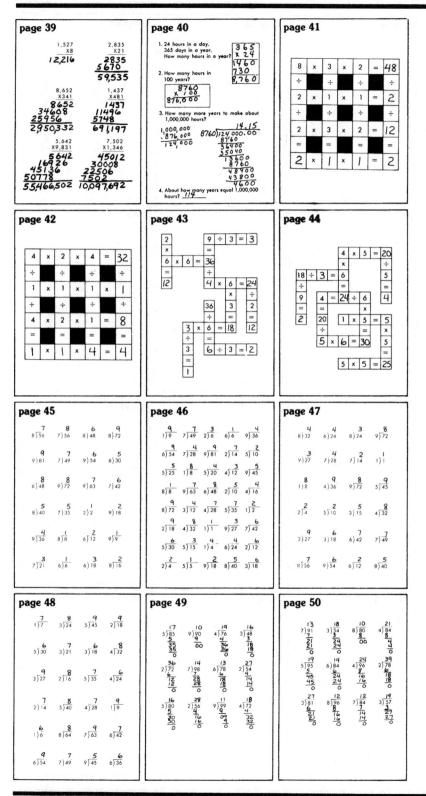

Solutions

0-88012-455-5

page 51

11 6)66	11 8)88	29 2)58	26 3)78
16 4)64	15 5)75	11 7)77	24 2)48
17 4)68	14 4)56	33 3)99	14 5)70

page 52

10 7)70	24 3)72	12 6)72	23 4)92
43 2)86	13 5)65	15 6)90	22 4)88
16 6)96	13 4)52	38 2)76	10 6)60

page 53

32 3)96	12 6)72	15 4)60	10 9)90
29 2)58	12 8)96	18 4)72	13 5)65
20 5)80	12 7)84	17 4)68	17 3)51
11 9)99	19 4)76	10 8)80	18 3)54
11 7)77	12 5)60	11 8)88	13 6)78

page 54

16 ÷ 2 = **8**   14 ÷ 2 = **7**

24 ÷ 2 = **12**   18 ÷ 2 = **9**

56 ÷ 2 = **28**   88 ÷ 2 = **44**

48 ÷ 2 = **24**   36 ÷ 2 = **18**

42 ÷ 2 = **21**   96 ÷ 2 = **48**

78 ÷ 2 = **39**   38 ÷ 2 = **19**

page 55

82 3)246	61 8)488	91 6)546
92 4)368	21 6)126	72 3)216
71 5)355	63 3)189	41 6)246

page 56

42 4)168	51 8)408	81 4)324
93 2)186	60 9)540	61 7)427
61 5)305	40 6)240	81 6)486

page 57

23 6)138	342 2)684	157 5)785
51 9)459	75 8)600	29 7)203
89 6)534	45 4)180	98 3)294
26 8)208	144 2)288	89 4)356

page 58

Germany	177 ÷ 3	59
Japan	273 ÷ 3	91
Italy	294 ÷ 3	98
Liechtenstein	171 ÷ 3	57
France	111 ÷ 3	37
Czechoslovakia	195 ÷ 3	65
Hungary	234 ÷ 3	78
El Salvador	144 ÷ 3	48
Haiti	102 ÷ 3	34
England	282 ÷ 3	94

page 59

745 3)2235	364 7)2548	226 9)2034
697 8)5576	887 4)3548	654 5)3270
359 4)1436	485 9)4365	713 6)4278

page 60

1. 3 feet in a pace.
5,280 feet in a mile
How many paces in a mile?

1760
3)5,280

2. How many paces in 100 miles?

1760
×100
176,000

3. How many paces in 500 miles?
176,000
× 5
880,000

4. About how many more miles to make about 1,000,000 paces?

1,000,000
− 880,000
120,000

68
1760)120,000
10560
14400
14080
320

5. About how many miles equal 1,000,000 paces? **568 miles**

page 61

23 14)322	12 23)276	11 45)495
12 78)936	19 37)703	15 62)930
18 52)936	11 82)902	10 90)900

page 62

11 84)924	15 66)990	35 28)980
24 41)984	12 69)828	13 76)988
15 56)840	22 45)990	40 24)960

0-88012-455-5

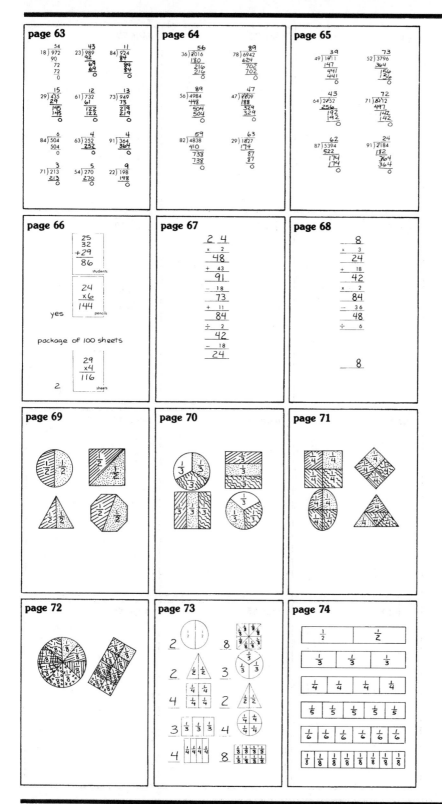

page 63

```
        54              43             11
   18) 972         23) 989        84) 924
       90              92             84
       72              69             84
       72              69             84
        0               0              0
```

```
        15              12             13
   29) 435         61) 732        73) 949
       29              61             73
      145             122            219
      145             122            219
        0               0              0
```

```
         6              4              4
   84) 504         63) 252        91) 364
       504            252            364
         0              0              0
```

```
         3              5              9
   71) 213         54) 270        22) 198
       213            270            198
         0              0              0
```

page 64

```
        56              89
   36) 2016        78) 6942
       180             624
       216             702
       216             702
         0               0
```

```
        89              47
   56) 4984        47) 2209
       448             188
       504             329
       504             329
         0               0
```

```
        59              63
   82) 4838        29) 1827
       410             174
       738              87
       738              87
         0               0
```

page 65

```
        39              73
   49) 1911        52) 3796
       147             364
       441             156
       441             156
         0               0
```

```
        43              72
   64) 2752        71) 5112
       256             497
       192             142
       192             142
         0               0
```

```
        62              24
   87) 5394        91) 2184
       522             182
       174             364
       174             364
         0               0
```

page 66

```
      25
      32
    + 29
      86
        students
```

```
      24
     x 6
     144
        pencils
```
yes

package of 100 sheets

```
      29
     x 4
     116
        sheets
```
2

page 67

```
     2 4
    x  2
     4 8
   +  4 3
     9 1
   -  1 8
     7 3
   +  1 1
     8 4
   ÷  2
     4 2
   -  1 8
     2 4
```

page 68

```
       8
    x  3
      24
   +  18
      42
    x  2
      84
   -  36
      48
   ÷   6
       8
```

page 69

page 70

page 71

page 72

page 73

```
2         8

2    3

4    2

3    4

4    8
```

page 74

© 2006 Frank Schaffer Publications

Solutions

0-88012-455-5

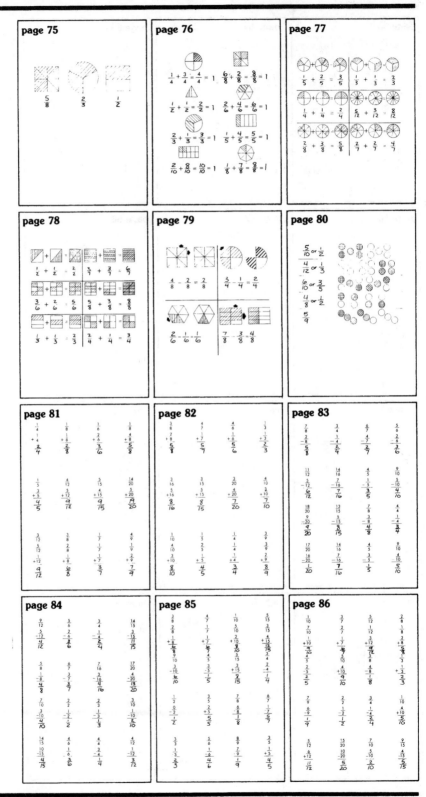

Solutions

True Number Sentences

Fill in the blanks so that all the number sentences are true.

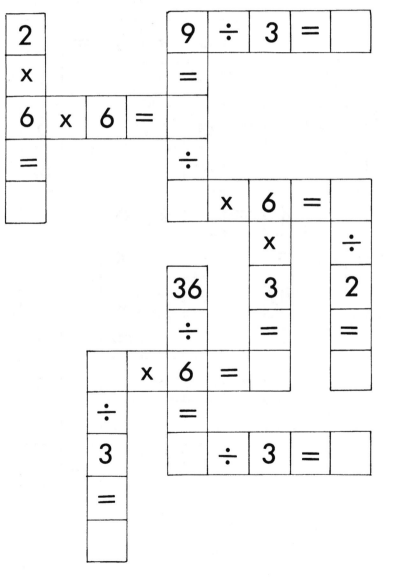

0-88012-455-5

True Number Sentences

Fill in the blanks so that all the number sentences are true.

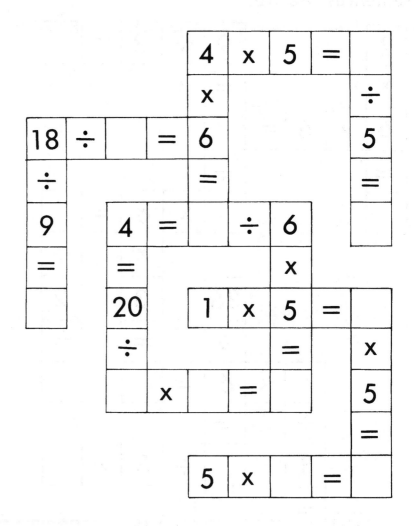

0-88012-455-5

Division

Find the quotients.

$8\overline{)56}$ $\quad$ $7\overline{)56}$ $\quad$ $8\overline{)48}$ $\quad$ $8\overline{)72}$

$9\overline{)81}$ $\quad$ $7\overline{)49}$ $\quad$ $9\overline{)54}$ $\quad$ $6\overline{)30}$

$6\overline{)48}$ $\quad$ $9\overline{)72}$ $\quad$ $9\overline{)63}$ $\quad$ $7\overline{)42}$

$8\overline{)40}$ $\quad$ $7\overline{)35}$ $\quad$ $2\overline{)2}$ $\quad$ $9\overline{)18}$

$9\overline{)36}$ $\quad$ $8\overline{)8}$ $\quad$ $6\overline{)12}$ $\quad$ $9\overline{)9}$

$7\overline{)21}$ $\quad$ $6\overline{)6}$ $\quad$ $6\overline{)18}$ $\quad$ $8\overline{)16}$

45

  0-88012-455-5

Division

Find the quotients

$1\overline{)9}$ $7\overline{)49}$ $2\overline{)6}$ $6\overline{)6}$ $9\overline{)36}$

$6\overline{)54}$ $7\overline{)28}$ $9\overline{)81}$ $2\overline{)14}$ $5\overline{)10}$

$5\overline{)25}$ $1\overline{)8}$ $5\overline{)20}$ $4\overline{)12}$ $9\overline{)45}$

$8\overline{)8}$ $9\overline{)63}$ $6\overline{)48}$ $2\overline{)10}$ $4\overline{)16}$

$8\overline{)72}$ $3\overline{)12}$ $4\overline{)28}$ $5\overline{)35}$ $1\overline{)2}$

$2\overline{)18}$ $4\overline{)32}$ $1\overline{)1}$ $9\overline{)27}$ $7\overline{)42}$

$5\overline{)30}$ $5\overline{)15}$ $1\overline{)4}$ $6\overline{)24}$ $2\overline{)12}$

$2\overline{)4}$ $5\overline{)5}$ $9\overline{)18}$ $8\overline{)40}$ $3\overline{)18}$

46

   0-88012-455-5

Division

Find the quotients.

8)32   6)24   8)24   9)72

9)27   7)28   7)14   1)1

1)8   4)36   9)72   5)45

2)4   5)10   3)15   4)32

3)27   3)18   6)42   7)49

8)56   9)54   6)12   8)40

47

    0-88012-455-5

Division

Find the quotients.

| $1\overline{)7}$ | $3\overline{)24}$ | $5\overline{)45}$ | $2\overline{)18}$ |

| $5\overline{)30}$ | $3\overline{)21}$ | $3\overline{)18}$ | $4\overline{)32}$ |

| $3\overline{)27}$ | $2\overline{)16}$ | $5\overline{)35}$ | $4\overline{)24}$ |

| $2\overline{)14}$ | $5\overline{)40}$ | $4\overline{)28}$ | $1\overline{)9}$ |

| $1\overline{)6}$ | $8\overline{)64}$ | $7\overline{)63}$ | $6\overline{)42}$ |

| $6\overline{)54}$ | $7\overline{)49}$ | $9\overline{)45}$ | $6\overline{)36}$ |

48

© 2006 Frank Schaffer Publications

0-88012-455-5

Division

Find the quotients.

$$6\overline{)72}$$

$$\begin{array}{r} 1 \\ 6\overline{)72} \\ \underline{6} \\ 1 \end{array}$$

$$\begin{array}{r} 1 \\ 6\overline{)72} \\ \underline{6} \\ 12 \end{array}$$

$$\begin{array}{r} 12 \\ 6\overline{)72} \\ \underline{6} \\ 12 \\ \underline{12} \\ 0 \end{array}$$

How to start

$$5\overline{)85} \qquad 9\overline{)90} \qquad 4\overline{)76} \qquad 3\overline{)48}$$

$$2\overline{)72} \qquad 7\overline{)98} \qquad 6\overline{)78} \qquad 2\overline{)54}$$

$$5\overline{)80} \qquad 2\overline{)56} \qquad 9\overline{)99} \qquad 4\overline{)72}$$

49

 0-88012-455-5

Division

Find the quotients.

Here's an example

$$4{\overline{)72}}$$

$$\begin{array}{r} 1 \\ 4{\overline{)72}} \\ 4 \\ \hline 3 \end{array}$$

$$\begin{array}{r} 18 \\ 4{\overline{)72}} \\ 4 \\ \hline 32 \end{array}$$

$$\begin{array}{r} 18 \\ 4{\overline{)72}} \\ 4 \\ \hline 32 \\ 32 \\ \hline 0 \end{array}$$

$$7{\overline{)91}} \qquad 3{\overline{)54}} \qquad 8{\overline{)80}} \qquad 4{\overline{)84}}$$

$$5{\overline{)95}} \qquad 6{\overline{)84}} \qquad 4{\overline{)96}} \qquad 2{\overline{)78}}$$

$$3{\overline{)81}} \qquad 8{\overline{)96}} \qquad 7{\overline{)84}} \qquad 3{\overline{)57}}$$

50

0-88012-455-5

Division

Find the quotients.

2)64	$\begin{array}{r} 3 \\ 2\overline{)64} \\ 6 \\ \hline 0 \end{array}$	$\begin{array}{r} 3 \\ 2\overline{)64} \\ 6 \\ \hline 04 \end{array}$	$\begin{array}{r} 32 \\ 2\overline{)64} \\ 6 \\ \hline 04 \\ 4 \\ \hline 0 \end{array}$

6)66   8)88   2)58   3)78

4)64   5)75   7)77   2)48

4)68   4)56   3)99   5)70

51

     0-88012-455-5

Division

Find the quotients.

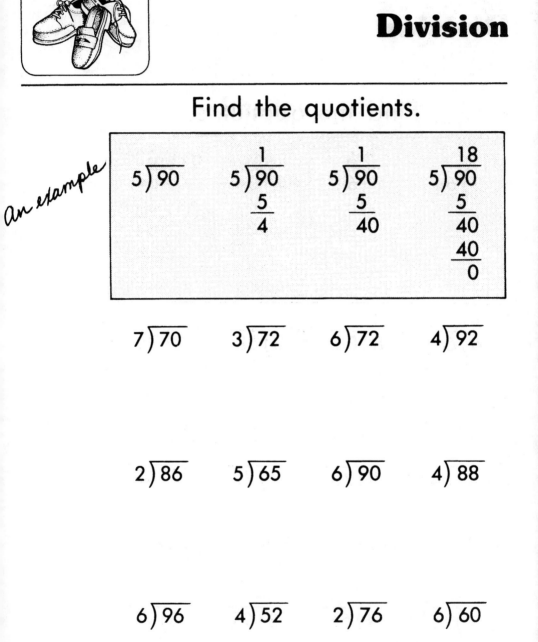

an example

$$5 \overline{)90}$$

$$\begin{array}{r} 1 \\ 5 \overline{)90} \\ 5 \\ \hline 4 \end{array}$$

$$\begin{array}{r} 1 \\ 5 \overline{)90} \\ 5 \\ \hline 40 \end{array}$$

$$\begin{array}{r} 18 \\ 5 \overline{)90} \\ 5 \\ \hline 40 \\ 40 \\ \hline 0 \end{array}$$

$$7 \overline{)70} \qquad 3 \overline{)72} \qquad 6 \overline{)72} \qquad 4 \overline{)92}$$

$$2 \overline{)86} \qquad 5 \overline{)65} \qquad 6 \overline{)90} \qquad 4 \overline{)88}$$

$$6 \overline{)96} \qquad 4 \overline{)52} \qquad 2 \overline{)76} \qquad 6 \overline{)60}$$

52

© 2006 Frank Schaffer Publications 0-88012-455-5

Division

Find the quotients.

```
      32
   3) 96        6) 72       4) 60       9) 90
      9
      6
      6
      0
```

2) 58   8) 96   4) 72   5) 65

5) 80   7) 84   4) 68   3) 51

9) 99   4) 76   8) 80   3) 54

7) 77   5) 60   8) 88   6) 78

53

  0-88012-455-5

The Cookie Maker

The Acme Cookie Middler is used to ice two cookies and stick them together. The Acme Cookie Middler takes two cookies and turns them into one. Figure how many cookies there will be when each group goes through the Acme Cookie Middler.

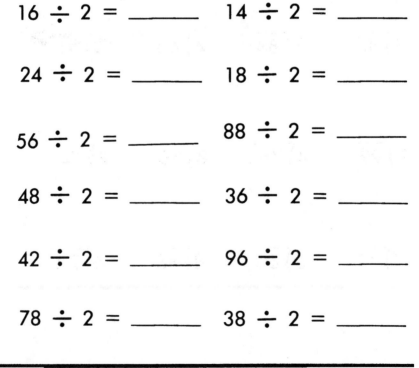

$16 \div 2 =$ _____ $14 \div 2 =$ _____

$24 \div 2 =$ _____ $18 \div 2 =$ _____

$56 \div 2 =$ _____ $88 \div 2 =$ _____

$48 \div 2 =$ _____ $36 \div 2 =$ _____

$42 \div 2 =$ _____ $96 \div 2 =$ _____

$78 \div 2 =$ _____ $38 \div 2 =$ _____

54

Division

Find the quotients.

```
        7          7          71
9)639   9)639      9)639      9)639        We did this
        63         63         63           one for you
        0          09         09
                              9
                              0
```

```
3)246      8)488      6)546
```

```
4)368      6)126      3)216
```

```
5)355      3)189      6)246
```

55

Division

Find the quotients.

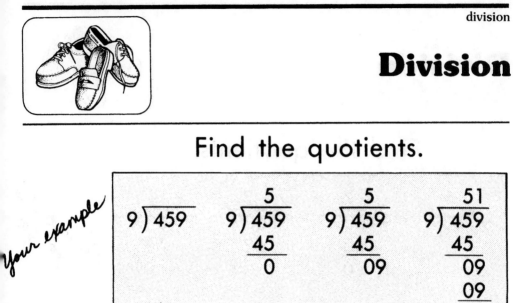

Your example

$$9\overline{)459}$$

$$\begin{array}{r} 5 \\ 9\overline{)459} \\ 45 \\ \hline 0 \end{array}$$

$$\begin{array}{r} 5 \\ 9\overline{)459} \\ 45 \\ \hline 09 \end{array}$$

$$\begin{array}{r} 51 \\ 9\overline{)459} \\ 45 \\ \hline 09 \\ 09 \\ \hline 0 \end{array}$$

$$4\overline{)168} \qquad 8\overline{)408} \qquad 4\overline{)324}$$

$$2\overline{)186} \qquad 9\overline{)540} \qquad 7\overline{)427}$$

$$5\overline{)305} \qquad 6\overline{)240} \qquad 6\overline{)486}$$

0-88012-455-5

Division

Find the quotients.

```
     23
6) 138
   12
   18
   18
    0
```

2) 684

5) 785

9) 459

8) 600

7) 203

6) 534

4) 180

3) 294

8) 208

2) 288

4) 356

0-88012-455-5

Stamp Collecting

Mr. Pletcher used to collect stamps. When he ran across his collection in a box at his parents' house, he decided to let his three children each have one third of the stamps. In order to be as fair as possible, he separated the stamps according to country. Each child could have one third of the stamps from each country. How many stamps did each child get from each country?

each share

Germany	177	_____
Japan	273	_____
Italy	294	_____
Liechtenstein	171	_____
France	111	_____
Czechoslovakia	195	_____
Hungary	234	_____
El Salvador	144	_____
Haiti	102	_____
England	282	_____

58

0-88012-455-5

Division

Find the quotients.

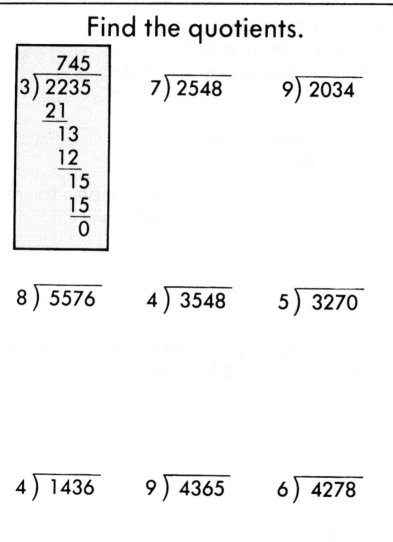

$$\begin{array}{r} 745 \\ 3\overline{)2235} \\ 21 \\ \hline 13 \\ 12 \\ \hline 15 \\ 15 \\ \hline 0 \end{array}$$

$7\overline{)2548}$

$9\overline{)2034}$

$8\overline{)5576}$

$4\overline{)3548}$

$5\overline{)3270}$

$4\overline{)1436}$

$9\overline{)4365}$

$6\overline{)4278}$

59

0-88012-455-5

Feet and Miles

1. 3 feet in a pace.
   5,280 feet in a mile
   How many paces in a mile?

   $3{\overline{\smash{)}\,5{,}280}}$

2. How many paces in
   100 miles?

3. How many paces in
   500 miles?

4. About how many more miles to make about 1,000,000 paces?

5. About how many miles equal 1,000,000 paces? _____

60

Division

Find the quotients.

$$13\overline{)728}\qquad 13\overline{)728}^{\,5}\atop{\underline{65}\atop 7}\qquad 13\overline{)728}^{\,5}\atop{\underline{65}\atop 78}\qquad 13\overline{)728}^{\,56}\atop{\underline{65}\atop{78\atop\underline{78}}}$$

Here's how

$14\overline{)322}$ $\qquad$ $23\overline{)276}$ $\qquad$ $45\overline{)495}$

$78\overline{)936}$ $\qquad$ $37\overline{)703}$ $\qquad$ $62\overline{)930}$

$52\overline{)936}$ $\qquad$ $82\overline{)902}$ $\qquad$ $90\overline{)900}$

61

 0-88012-455-5

Division

Find the quotients.

Here's an example

$$36 \overline{)864}$$

$$\begin{array}{r} 2 \\ 36 \overline{)864} \\ 72 \\ \hline 14 \end{array}$$

$$\begin{array}{r} 2 \\ 36 \overline{)864} \\ 72 \\ \hline 144 \end{array}$$

$$\begin{array}{r} 24 \\ 36 \overline{)864} \\ 72 \\ \hline 144 \\ 144 \\ \hline 0 \end{array}$$

$$84 \overline{)924} \qquad 66 \overline{)990} \qquad 28 \overline{)980}$$

$$41 \overline{)984} \qquad 69 \overline{)828} \qquad 76 \overline{)988}$$

$$56 \overline{)840} \qquad 45 \overline{)990} \qquad 24 \overline{)960}$$

62

0-88012-455-5

Division

Find the quotients.

$$
\begin{array}{r}
54 \\
18\overline{)972} \\
90 \\
\hline
72 \\
72 \\
\hline
0
\end{array}
$$

$23\overline{)989}$

$84\overline{)924}$

$29\overline{)435}$

$61\overline{)732}$

$73\overline{)949}$

$$
\begin{array}{r}
6 \\
84\overline{)504} \\
504 \\
\hline
0
\end{array}
$$

$63\overline{)252}$

$91\overline{)364}$

$71\overline{)213}$

$54\overline{)270}$

$22\overline{)198}$

63

0-88012-455-5

Division

Find the quotients.

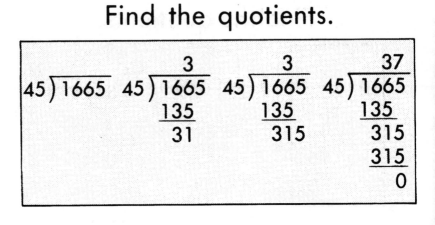

$$45 \overline{) 1665} \qquad 45 \overline{) \begin{array}{c} 3 \\ 1665 \\ \underline{135} \\ 31 \end{array}} \qquad 45 \overline{) \begin{array}{c} 3 \\ 1665 \\ \underline{135} \\ 315 \end{array}} \qquad 45 \overline{) \begin{array}{c} 37 \\ 1665 \\ \underline{135} \\ 315 \\ \underline{315} \\ 0 \end{array}}$$

$$36 \overline{) 2016} \qquad\qquad 78 \overline{) 6942}$$

$$56 \overline{) 4984} \qquad\qquad 47 \overline{) 2209}$$

$$82 \overline{) 4838} \qquad\qquad 29 \overline{) 1827}$$

0-88012-455-5

Division

Find the quotients.

$$
\begin{array}{r}
68\overline{)2856}
\end{array}
\qquad
\begin{array}{r}
4 \\
68\overline{)2856} \\
272 \\
\hline
13
\end{array}
\qquad
\begin{array}{r}
42 \\
68\overline{)2856} \\
272 \\
\hline
136
\end{array}
\qquad
\begin{array}{r}
42 \\
68\overline{)2856} \\
272 \\
\hline
136 \\
136 \\
\hline
0
\end{array}
\qquad \textit{an example}
$$

$49\overline{)1911}$ $\qquad$ $52\overline{)3796}$

$64\overline{)2752}$ $\qquad$ $71\overline{)5112}$

$87\overline{)5394}$ $\qquad$ $91\overline{)2184}$

65

0-88012-455-5

Pencils and Paper

There are three fourth grades in the Crestview Elementary School. The classes have the following enrollments: Mrs. Winston's class — 25, Mr. Wilson's — 32, Ms. James'— 29. How many fourth graders are there?

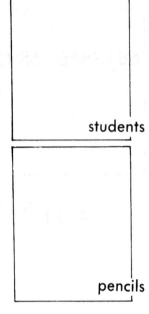

students

There is a small school store. In the store are six boxes of pencils. Each box contains 24 pencils. How many pencils are there in the school store?

If everyone in the fourth grade needed to buy a pencil, could they all buy them at the school store?

pencils

The school store carries two kinds of notebook paper. One package contains 20 sheets and costs a quarter. The other package contains 100 sheets and sells for $.98. Which package is the better buy?

Ms. James has a project that will require four pieces of paper for each child. How many of the large packages of paper must they buy? _____ packages.

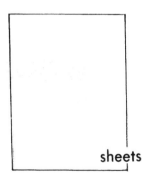

sheets

66

0-88012-455-5

Number Tricks

Try number trick number 1.

1. Write any two-digit number:_____ _____

2. Double it: . . . . $\underline{\times \quad 2}$

3. Add 43: . . . . $\underline{+ \quad 43}$

4. Subtract 18: . . . . $\underline{- \quad 18}$

5. Add 11: . . . . $\underline{+ \quad 11}$

6. Divide by 2: . . . . $\underline{\div \quad 2}$

7. Subtract 18: . . . . $\underline{- \quad 18}$

If you did not make any mistakes, this is your original number.

67

     0-88012-455-5

Number Tricks

Try number trick number 2.

1. Write your age: .... _____

2. Multiply your age by 3: ... x   3

   _____

3. Add 18: .... +   18

   _____

4. Multiply by 2: x   2

   _____

5. Subtract 36: .... —   3 6

   _____

6. Divide by 6: .... ÷   6

   _____

Keep up the good work!

You have finished

Step 3

If you did not make any mistakes, your age will appear on this line. .... _____

0-88012-455-5

Fractions

> When an object is divided into 2 equal parts, each part is called one half. We usually write one half with numerals that look like this:
>
> ½
>
> This kind of numeral is called a **fraction**.

Each shape below has been divided into 2 equal parts.

Label each part ½.

Color ½ of each shape red.

Color ½ of each shape blue.

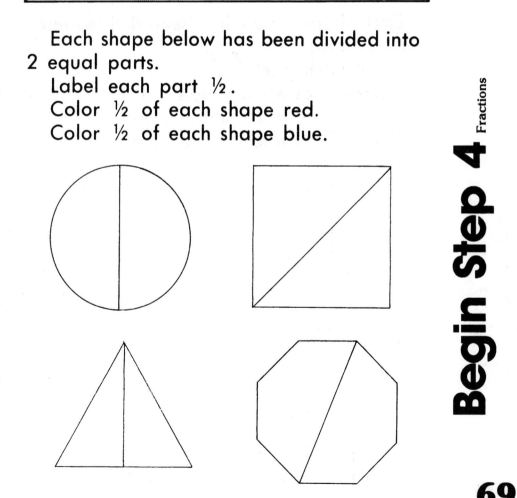

Begin Step 4 Fractions

69

Fractions

Read this first

When an object is divided into 3 equal parts, each part is called one third. We usually write one third with numerals that look like this:

$\frac{1}{3}$

This kind of numeral is called a **fraction**.

Each shape below has been divided into 3 equal parts.

Label each part $\frac{1}{3}$.

Color $\frac{1}{3}$ of each shape red.

Color $\frac{1}{3}$ of each shape blue.

Color $\frac{1}{3}$ of each shape green.

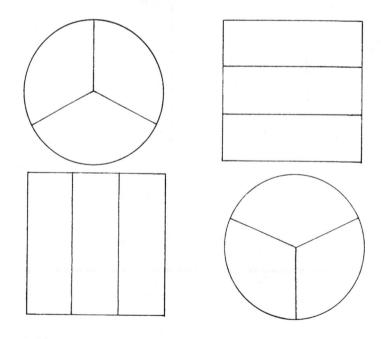

70

 0-88012-455-5

Fractions

When an object is divided into 4 equal parts, each part is called one fourth. We usually write one fourth with numerals that look like this:

¼

This kind of numeral is called a **fraction**.

Each shape below has been divided into 4 equal parts.
Label each part ¼.
Color ¼ of each shape red.
Color ¼ of each shape blue.
Color ¼ of each shape green.
Color ¼ of each shape yellow.

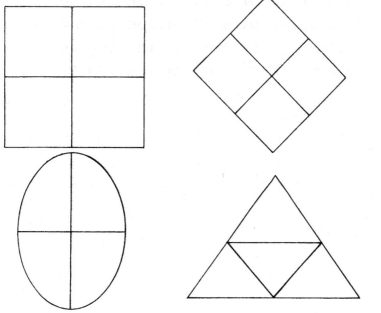

71

Fractions

study this first

When an object is divided into 8 equal parts, each part is called one eighth. We usually write one eighth with numerals that look like this:

⅛

This kind of numeral is called a **fraction**.

Each shape below has been divided into 8 equal parts.

Label each part ⅛.

Color ⅛ of each shape red.

Color ⅛ of each shape blue.

Color ⅛ of each shape green.

Color ⅛ of each shape orange.

Color ⅛ of each shape purple.

Color ⅛ of each shape yellow.

Color ⅛ of each shape brown.

Color ⅛ of each shape black.

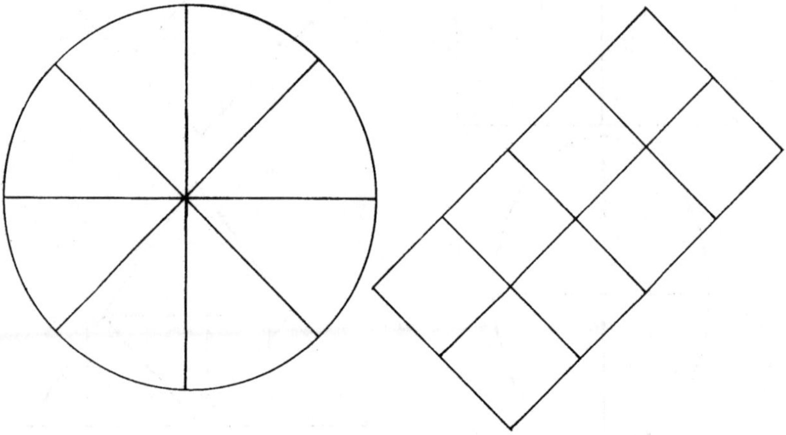

72

0-88012-455-5

Fractions

Write the numeral that tells how many equal parts are in each shape.

Label each part with the correct fraction: ½, ⅓, ¼, or ⅛.

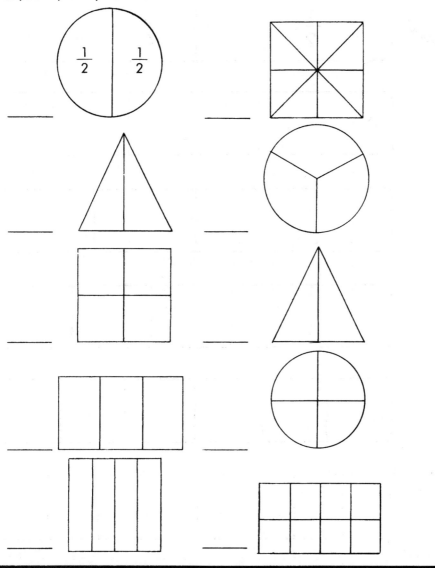

0-88012-455-5

Fractions

Label each part of each strip with the correct fraction.

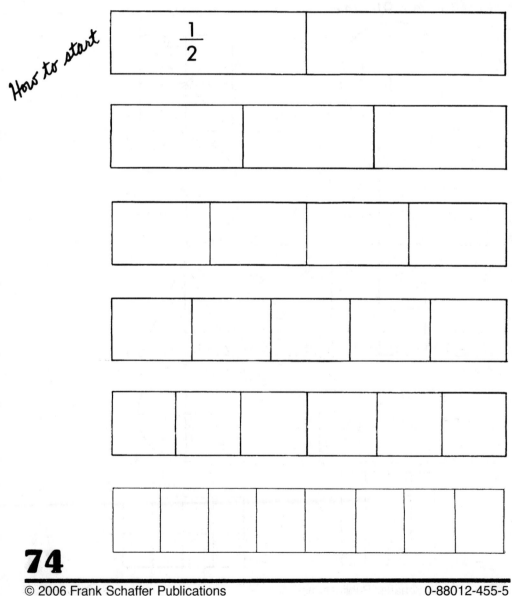

$$\frac{1}{2}$$

© 2006 Frank Schaffer Publications   0-88012-455-5

Fractions

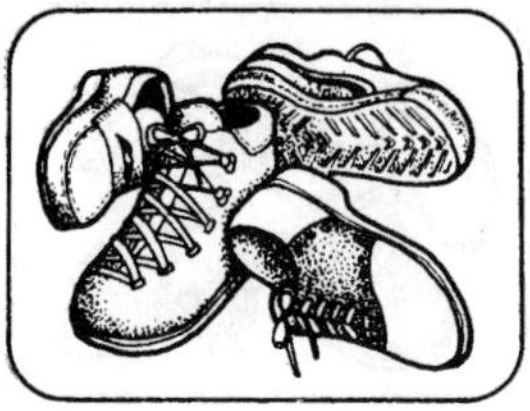

Fractions tell two things about objects that have been divided into parts.

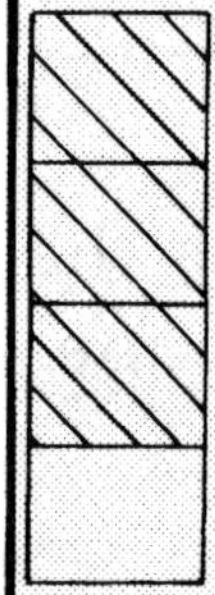

$\frac{\ }{4}$ → The numeral below the line tells how many parts are in the whole object.

$\frac{3}{4}$ → The numeral above the line tells how many parts of the whole are going to be used at the moment.

Study this first

These fractions tell about the shaded part of each shape.

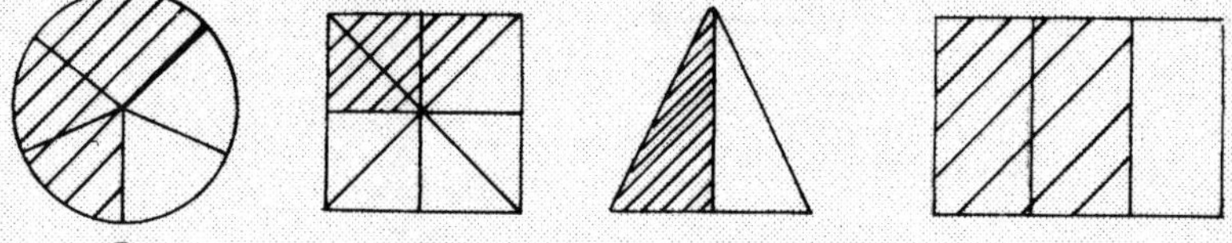

$\frac{3}{5}$ $\frac{3}{8}$ $\frac{1}{2}$ $\frac{2}{3}$

Write the correct fraction for each shaded drawing.

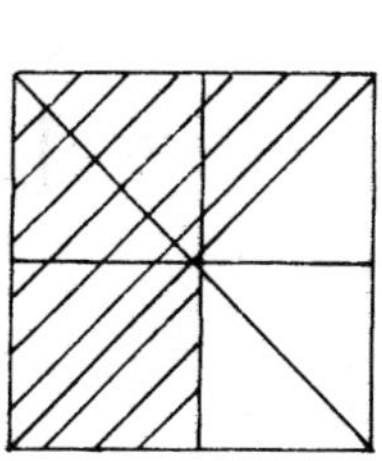

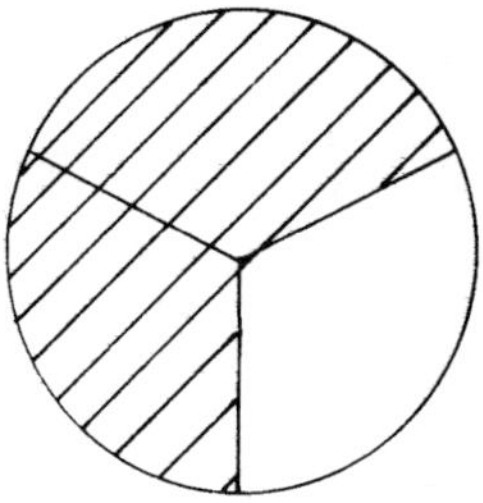

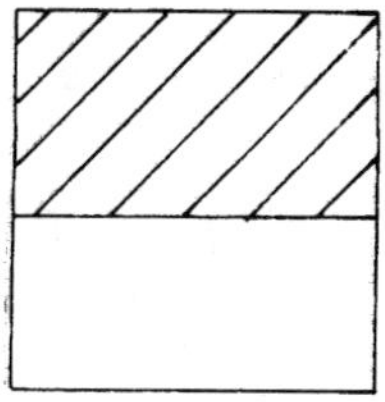

— — —

0-88012-455-5

Fractions

Study each shape.

Write a fraction that tells what part of the whole is shaded.

Write a fraction that tells what part of the whole is not shaded.

Write a fraction that combines both the shaded and unshaded parts of the shape.

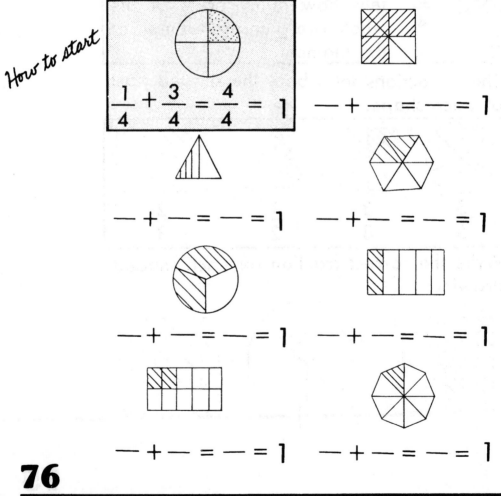

How to start

$$\frac{1}{4} + \frac{3}{4} = \frac{4}{4} = 1$$

$$— + — = — = 1$$

$$— + — = — = 1 \qquad — + — = — = 1$$

$$— + — = — = 1 \qquad — + — = — = 1$$

$$— + — = — = 1 \qquad — + — = — = 1$$

76

0-88012-455-5

Fractions

Write the fraction that tells what part of each shape is shaded.

Combine the shaded parts of each pair of shaded shapes.

Shade the third shape and write the correct fraction.

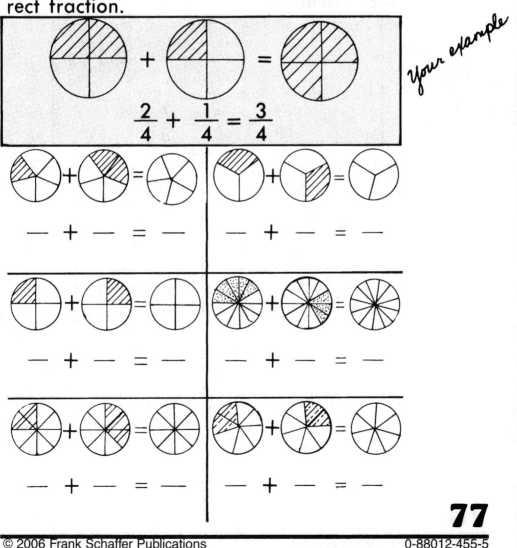

$$\frac{2}{4} + \frac{1}{4} = \frac{3}{4}$$

Your example

— + — = —

— + — = —

— + — = —

— + — = —

— + — = —

— + — = —

77

0-88012-455-5

Fractions

Write the fraction that tells what part of each shape is shaded.

Combine the shaded parts of each pair of shaded shapes.

Shade the third shape and write the correct fraction.

We did this one for you

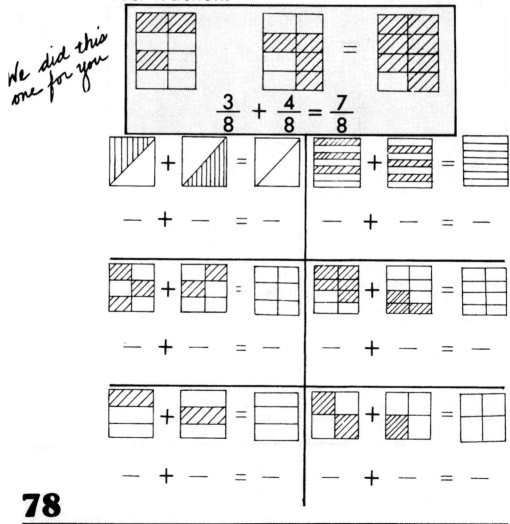

$$\frac{3}{8} + \frac{4}{8} = \frac{7}{8}$$

— + — = —   — + — = —

— + — = —   — + — = —

— + — = —   — + — = —

78

          0-88012-455-5

fractions

Fractions

Study each shape.
Write a fraction that tells what part has been shaded.
Write another fraction that tells how many parts are to be subtracted.
Subtract and write a fraction that tells what part will be left.
Shade the shape on the right to show what part will be left.

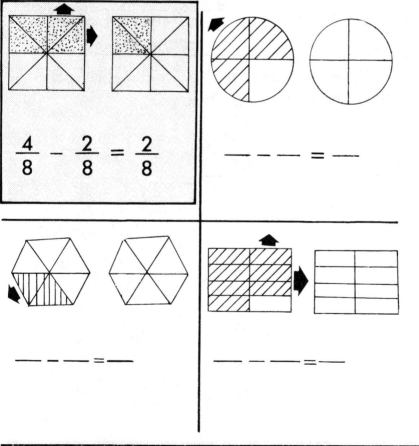

$$\frac{4}{8} - \frac{2}{8} = \frac{2}{8}$$

$$\underline{} - \underline{} = \underline{}$$

$$\underline{} - \underline{} = \underline{}$$

$$\underline{} - \underline{} = \underline{}$$

79

0-88012-455-5

Fractions

Fractions can be used to tell about selected objects in a set of objects.

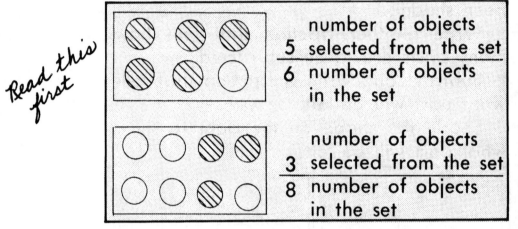

$\dfrac{5}{6}$ number of objects selected from the set / number of objects in the set

$\dfrac{3}{8}$ number of objects selected from the set / number of objects in the set

Write a fraction that tells what part of each set has been shaded.

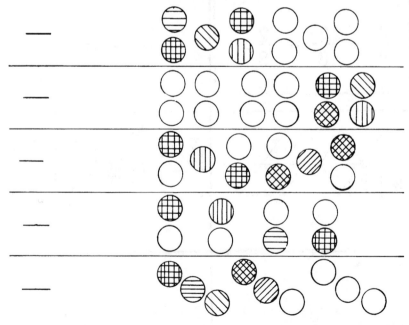

_____

_____

_____

_____

_____

80

Adding Fractions

Find the sums.

$$\frac{1}{4}$$
$$+\frac{1}{4}$$

$$\frac{1}{8}$$
$$+\frac{1}{8}$$

$$\frac{1}{6}$$
$$+\frac{2}{6}$$

$$\frac{1}{8}$$
$$+\frac{4}{8}$$

$$\frac{1}{5}$$
$$+\frac{3}{5}$$

$$\frac{4}{12}$$
$$+\frac{5}{12}$$

$$\frac{5}{15}$$
$$+\frac{4}{15}$$

$$\frac{14}{20}$$
$$+\frac{5}{20}$$

$$\frac{3}{12}$$
$$\frac{5}{12}$$
$$+\frac{1}{12}$$

$$\frac{3}{8}$$
$$\frac{2}{8}$$
$$+\frac{1}{8}$$

$$\frac{1}{7}$$
$$\frac{1}{7}$$
$$+\frac{1}{7}$$

$$\frac{4}{9}$$
$$\frac{1}{9}$$
$$+\frac{2}{9}$$

81

0-88012-455-5

Adding Fractions

Find the sums.

$$\frac{3}{8} + \frac{2}{8}$$ $$\frac{4}{7} + \frac{1}{7}$$ $$\frac{4}{6} + \frac{1}{6}$$ $$\frac{1}{3} + \frac{1}{3}$$

$$\frac{3}{16} + \frac{5}{16}$$ $$\frac{3}{15} + \frac{5}{15}$$ $$\frac{3}{20} + \frac{4}{20}$$ $$\frac{4}{10} + \frac{3}{10}$$

$$\frac{1}{10} + \frac{4}{10} + \frac{3}{10}$$ $$\frac{1}{5} + \frac{2}{5} + \frac{1}{5}$$ $$\frac{1}{4} + \frac{1}{4} + \frac{1}{4}$$ $$\frac{3}{9} + \frac{3}{9} + \frac{2}{9}$$

82

    0-88012-455-5

Subtracting Fractions

Find the differences.

$$\frac{7}{8} - \frac{2}{8}$$ $$\frac{3}{4} - \frac{1}{4}$$ $$\frac{6}{7} - \frac{4}{7}$$ $$\frac{5}{6} - \frac{2}{6}$$

$$\frac{11}{12} - \frac{5}{12}$$ $$\frac{14}{16} - \frac{7}{16}$$ $$\frac{4}{5} - \frac{1}{5}$$ $$\frac{9}{10} - \frac{5}{10}$$

$$\frac{18}{20} - \frac{9}{20}$$ $$\frac{13}{15} - \frac{5}{15}$$ $$\frac{7}{8} - \frac{3}{8}$$ $$\frac{4}{4} - \frac{1}{4}$$

$$\frac{17}{20} - \frac{16}{20}$$ $$\frac{14}{16} - \frac{7}{16}$$ $$\frac{4}{5} - \frac{3}{5}$$ $$\frac{9}{10} - \frac{4}{10}$$

83

Subtracting Fractions

Find the differences.

$$\begin{array}{r} \frac{9}{12} \\ -\frac{5}{12} \\ \hline \end{array} \qquad \begin{array}{r} \frac{5}{6} \\ -\frac{2}{6} \\ \hline \end{array} \qquad \begin{array}{r} \frac{3}{4} \\ -\frac{1}{4} \\ \hline \end{array} \qquad \begin{array}{r} \frac{14}{15} \\ -\frac{3}{15} \\ \hline \end{array}$$

$$\begin{array}{r} \frac{5}{8} \\ -\frac{1}{8} \\ \hline \end{array} \qquad \begin{array}{r} \frac{6}{7} \\ -\frac{3}{7} \\ \hline \end{array} \qquad \begin{array}{r} \frac{7}{16} \\ -\frac{3}{16} \\ \hline \end{array} \qquad \begin{array}{r} \frac{17}{20} \\ -\frac{4}{20} \\ \hline \end{array}$$

$$\begin{array}{r} \frac{7}{10} \\ -\frac{3}{10} \\ \hline \end{array} \qquad \begin{array}{r} \frac{2}{2} \\ -\frac{1}{2} \\ \hline \end{array} \qquad \begin{array}{r} \frac{2}{3} \\ -\frac{1}{3} \\ \hline \end{array} \qquad \begin{array}{r} \frac{3}{10} \\ -\frac{1}{10} \\ \hline \end{array}$$

$$\begin{array}{r} \frac{14}{15} \\ -\frac{10}{15} \\ \hline \end{array} \qquad \begin{array}{r} \frac{4}{6} \\ -\frac{1}{6} \\ \hline \end{array} \qquad \begin{array}{r} \frac{4}{4} \\ -\frac{3}{4} \\ \hline \end{array} \qquad \begin{array}{r} \frac{4}{12} \\ -\frac{1}{12} \\ \hline \end{array}$$

84

 0-88012-455-5

Adding and
Subtracting Fractions

Find the sums and differences.

$$\begin{array}{r} \frac{3}{8} \\ \frac{2}{8} \\ +\frac{1}{8} \\ \hline \end{array} \qquad \begin{array}{r} \frac{4}{7} \\ \frac{1}{7} \\ +\frac{1}{7} \\ \hline \end{array} \qquad \begin{array}{r} \frac{1}{10} \\ \frac{5}{10} \\ +\frac{2}{10} \\ \hline \end{array} \qquad \begin{array}{r} \frac{5}{15} \\ \frac{3}{15} \\ +\frac{4}{15} \\ \hline \end{array}$$

$$\begin{array}{r} \frac{9}{10} \\ \frac{3}{10} \\ -\frac{}{} \\ \hline \end{array} \qquad \begin{array}{r} \frac{4}{5} \\ \frac{3}{5} \\ -\frac{}{} \\ \hline \end{array} \qquad \begin{array}{r} \frac{5}{15} \\ \frac{3}{15} \\ +\frac{}{} \\ \hline \end{array} \qquad \begin{array}{r} \frac{3}{4} \\ \frac{2}{4} \\ -\frac{}{} \\ \hline \end{array}$$

$$\begin{array}{r} \frac{1}{2} \\ \frac{0}{2} \\ -\frac{}{} \\ \hline \end{array} \qquad \begin{array}{r} \frac{3}{5} \\ \frac{2}{5} \\ +\frac{}{} \\ \hline \end{array} \qquad \begin{array}{r} \frac{7}{8} \\ \frac{6}{8} \\ -\frac{}{} \\ \hline \end{array} \qquad \begin{array}{r} \frac{6}{7} \\ \frac{1}{7} \\ -\frac{}{} \\ \hline \end{array}$$

$$\begin{array}{r} \frac{3}{3} \\ \frac{1}{3} \\ -\frac{}{} \\ \hline \end{array} \qquad \begin{array}{r} \frac{5}{6} \\ \frac{1}{6} \\ -\frac{}{} \\ \hline \end{array} \qquad \begin{array}{r} \frac{8}{9} \\ \frac{7}{9} \\ -\frac{}{} \\ \hline \end{array} \qquad \begin{array}{r} \frac{3}{5} \\ \frac{1}{5} \\ +\frac{}{} \\ \hline \end{array}$$

85

  0-88012-455-5

Adding and Subtracting Fractions

Find the sums and differences.

$$\begin{array}{r} \frac{1}{10} \\ \frac{7}{10} \\ +\frac{1}{10} \\ \hline \end{array} \qquad \begin{array}{r} \frac{3}{7} \\ \frac{2}{7} \\ +\frac{1}{7} \\ \hline \end{array} \qquad \begin{array}{r} \frac{5}{12} \\ \frac{1}{12} \\ +\frac{3}{12} \\ \hline \end{array} \qquad \begin{array}{r} \frac{2}{8} \\ \frac{1}{8} \\ +\frac{2}{8} \\ \hline \end{array}$$

$$\begin{array}{r} \frac{4}{5} \\ \frac{2}{5} \\ -\frac{2}{5} \\ \hline \end{array} \qquad \begin{array}{r} \frac{5}{10} \\ \frac{4}{10} \\ +\frac{4}{10} \\ \hline \end{array} \qquad \begin{array}{r} \frac{5}{8} \\ \frac{4}{8} \\ -\frac{4}{8} \\ \hline \end{array} \qquad \begin{array}{r} \frac{1}{3} \\ \frac{1}{3} \\ +\frac{1}{3} \\ \hline \end{array}$$

You're finished
Way to go!

$$\begin{array}{r} \frac{7}{9} \\ \frac{6}{9} \\ -\frac{6}{9} \\ \hline \end{array} \qquad \begin{array}{r} \frac{2}{2} \\ \frac{1}{2} \\ -\frac{1}{2} \\ \hline \end{array} \qquad \begin{array}{r} \frac{3}{4} \\ \frac{1}{4} \\ -\frac{1}{4} \\ \hline \end{array} \qquad \begin{array}{r} \frac{1}{10} \\ \frac{4}{10} \\ +\frac{4}{10} \\ \hline \end{array}$$

You have finished

this Book

$$\begin{array}{r} \frac{5}{12} \\ \frac{6}{12} \\ +\frac{6}{12} \\ \hline \end{array} \qquad \begin{array}{r} \frac{15}{20} \\ \frac{10}{20} \\ -\frac{10}{20} \\ \hline \end{array} \qquad \begin{array}{r} \frac{7}{10} \\ \frac{5}{10} \\ -\frac{5}{10} \\ \hline \end{array} \qquad \begin{array}{r} \frac{9}{15} \\ \frac{4}{15} \\ -\frac{4}{15} \\ \hline \end{array}$$

86

© 2006 Frank Schaffer Publications 0-88012-455-5